Night Mind™

by pro bookmark™

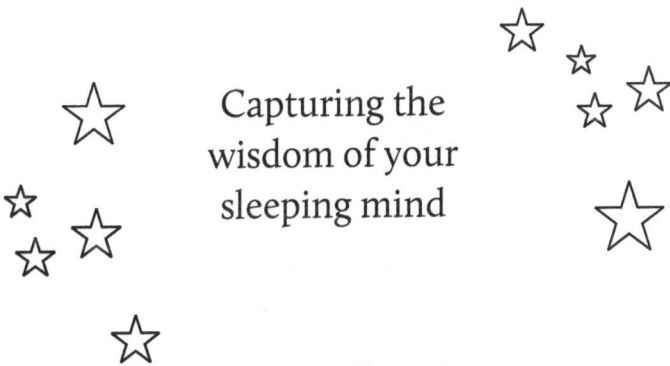

Capturing the
wisdom of your
sleeping mind

Dr. Roger D. Smith
with Tonya K. Smith

Night Mind by ProBookmark: Capturing the wisdom of your sleeping mind

Modelbenders Press books may be purchased for business and promotional use or for special sales. For information please contact the publisher.

ProBookmark™, Night Mind™, and Dream Seed™ are trademarks of Modelbenders LLC.

PRINTED IN THE UNITED STATES OF AMERICA

Visit our web site at www.modelbenders.com

Designed by Adina Cucicov at Flamingo Designs
Cover image: © Dmitriy Melnikov—Fotolia.com

The Library of Congress has cataloged the paperback edition as follows:

Smith, Roger
    Night Mind by ProBookmark: Capturing the wisdom of your sleeping mind.
    Roger Smith. – 1st ed.
    1. Body, Mind & Spirit: Dreams 2. Self-Help: Dreams—General
    3. Psychology: Creative Ability
    I. Roger Smith II. Title

ISBN 978-0-9843993-6-9

ProBookmark™ Series

ProBookmark™:
Capturing the riches you read for a lifetime

ProBookmark™ for Bible Study:
Capturing your study of the Bible for a lifetime

Daily Goals Journal by ProBookmark™:
Achieving your goals through daily action

Night Mind™ by ProBookmark™:
Capturing the wisdom of your sleeping mind

Night Mind™
by ProBookmark™

ALL DAY LONG YOU encounter challenges and problems in your work, home, school, professional, and family endeavors. Your mind takes in huge streams of information and makes decisions about how to handle each of them. In most cases, you see a problem and your mind delivers a solution in a few seconds. Your marvelous brain somehow rearranges everything that it knows and extracts the important points in the time it takes you to blink your eyes, take a breath, and speak a few words. Then it is off to the next problem.

But when you move on, your mind continues solving earlier problems, mulling them over and often finding better solutions than the one that jumped out in the first few seconds. Hours later you may return to a problem with a new and better approach because your mind was able to spend more time and energy creating a solution. It was able to consider the problem from a distance without the immediate pressure from people or machines that needed a solution immediately.

Your mind can do all of this "rethinking" about old problems while you are working on new problems. If you can do this while you are awake and busy, what can your mind do when it is asleep and totally free to work on a problem for as long as necessary?

When you lay down exhausted for the night, your mind does not shut off. It is busy putting everything that you did and thought during the day into order. Your Night Mind™ is moving things around in your brain and storing images so they can be remembered for years to come. In the process, it also trips over older memories that are stored next door. Together the old and new come tumbling into your dreams as original images, exciting adventures, terrifying nightmares, and confusing messages.

Inside all of this clutter there are often brilliant solutions to your current problems. You can pick out those solutions and put them to work if you will just invest a little time and effort before you jump into the new day. Each morning you need just a few minutes to calmly recall your dreams, capture the images, and extract the buried messages inside them.

Night Mind™ by ProBookmark™ is just one tool to help you do this. Each page will help you capture the important people, objects, events, and feelings that are in your dreams. You will identify your role in that dream and write one explanation for its meaning. This journal is meant to be kept by your bedside with a pen and a light so you can capture your dream images before they fade away like the morning fog.

You should also be aware of two important facts about your dreams. First, situations that are very deep and very important may trigger a sequence of recurring dreams. Your mind may spend many nights trying to work out a solution to a particularly difficult problem. Each morning you should tag a recurring dream so you can compare it to previous nights. Are you making progress toward solving it? Big issues may require many repetitions. But some problems have no solution. Your night mind is very persistent and will try to solve the same problem over and over again, even if it is an unsolvable problem. In that case, your night mind may need your conscious help to let go of the problem so you can move on in your waking life and your sleeping life.

Second, your mind sits atop a physical body and shares the same chemistry. Sometimes the problem that your night mind is trying to solve is simply how to digest a supreme pizza with extra sausage. The foods that you eat during the day can have a direct impact on your dreams. Sometimes a particularly amazing dream is the direct result of a particularly amazing meal. Try not to spend too much time and effort decoding the meaning of last night's dinner.

Now let's get to work harvesting the insightful solutions and new ideas that your night mind comes up with when you are not in conscious control.

How to use Night Mind™ by ProBookmark™

YOU CAN LOOK AT this goal journal and understand instantly what you are supposed to do with it. The format is self-explanatory. But here are some tips that will help you get the most out of this powerful tool.

Dream Description

Upon waking, immediately start recording the images, events, and feelings of the dream. It is important to capture the details before they fade and become lost forever. Once that is done you can work on the Dream Tracker section.

Dream Tracker

1. **Title.** Give your dream a title. What image or feeling was most prominent in the dream? The title will also help you connect several dreams together to see what progress you are making on a specific idea.

2. **Date.** Enter today's date and the day of the week. Look for patterns to your dreams based on week nights and weekends.

3. **Recurring.** Is this a recurring dream? Is there a pattern to the nights on which the dream recurs?

4. **Events.** What happened the day before the dream? Was there a particularly big event that may have influenced your dream?

5. **Food.** Jot down any unusual foods that you had yesterday. Was the dream was caused by a change in digestion rather than a change in life problems?

6. **Dream Seed™.** It is possible for you to give some guidance to your night mind by seeding it with a problem, picture, or question immediately before going to bed. You cannot control the night mind like you do your daily thoughts, but you can nudge it in a particular direction. Dream Seeds™ are most effective if they are expressed as images, action scenes, or short questions. Remember that your mind is full of useful information; the seed is just a pointer to send your night mind to that much bigger pool if it chooses to work on the problem you have suggested.

7. **My Role.** Were you personally playing a role in this dream? If so, what was it and who were you? In many dreams you will find yourself acting as a different person. There can be meaning in this role reversal.

8. **People.** Who was in the dream? Some people you will know by name, others will be strangers with a specific personality or image to convey.

9. **Objects.** What objects were prominent in the dream? Most dreams have a setting just like a movie or book. Objects may just be the props needed to support the story, or they may be very important players in the story itself.

10. **Events.** What was happening? Dream actions are often the solution to a puzzle you are trying to solve in the real world. Usually, the dream cannot be applied literally to a problem, but carries figurative message that can be translated.

11. **Feelings.** How did you feel in the dream? In most cases a dream is built inside of a feeling. So it is not your character that has a feeling, but the entire dream that is generating the feeling.

12. **Meaning.** Give your first impression of what this dream means to you. This will be your first interpretation. You can return to the images later with additional meaning.

13. **Action.** How will you apply the message in the dream to your daily life?

14. **Importance.** How important do you think this dream was? You do not solve difficult and meaningful problems every night. Was this a five star dream or a one star dream relative to your life?

Recurring Dreams

Periodically you should make a list of your recurring dreams. Most people have only one or two dreams which seem to be the same story repeated over and over. But, if you look at your dream tracker records you will see common themes and objects running through many different stories. Your list of recurring dreams should include the people, objects, actions, and feelings that recur in your dreams. These may appear in different stories, but they are still a case of recurrence which you should explore.

Celebrate & Repeat

This journal contains 100 pages for nightly dreams, along with several recurring dream lists. If you completely fill out one journal, then you are the kind of person who both enjoys and finds real benefit in harvesting the wisdom and insight of your night mind. When you finish an entire journal, celebrate the riches you have uncovered, then get another *Night Mind*™ journal and keep marching forward.

You are on a path to enriching your waking life with the power of your night mind. This journal is just one tool to help you get there.

Best Wishes,
Roger Smith

Dream Description

date ....

....

....

....

....

....

....

....

....

....

....

....

....

....

....

....

....

....

....

....

....

....

....

....

Dream Tracker

Night Mind™
by bookmark™ [pro]

title ....

date .... recurring ☐ Yes ☐ No

DAY BEFORE

events ....

food ....

dream seed™ ....

IN DREAM

my role ....

people ....

objects ....

events ....

feelings ....

MEANING

....

....

....

....

....

ACTION

....

....

....

2   importance ☆☆☆☆☆

Dream Description

date ....

....

....

....

....

....

....

....

....

....

....

....

....

....

....

....

....

....

....

....

....

....

....

Dream Tracker

Night Mind™
by pro bookmark™

title ....

date .... recurring ☐ Yes ☐ No

DAY BEFORE

events ....

food ....

dream seed™ ....

IN DREAM

my role ....

people ....

objects ....

events ....

feelings ....

MEANING

....

....

....

....

....

ACTION

....

....

....

4   importance ☆☆☆☆☆

Dream Description

Night Mind™
by bookmark™ [pro]

date ....

....

....

....

....

....

....

....

....

....

....

....

....

....

....

....

....

....

....

....

....

....

....

....

....

....

....

....

Dream Tracker

title ....

date .... recurring ☐ Yes ☐ No

DAY BEFORE

events ....

food ....

dream seed™ ....

IN DREAM

my role ....

people ....

objects ....

events ....

feelings ....

MEANING

....

....

....

....

....

ACTION

....

....

....

6   importance ☆☆☆☆☆

Dream Description

date ....

....

....

....

....

....

....

....

....

....

....

....

....

....

....

....

....

....

....

....

....

....

....

Dream Tracker

title ....

date ....   recurring   ❐ Yes ❐ No

DAY BEFORE

events ....

food ....

dream seed™ ....

IN DREAM

my role ....

people ....

objects ....

events ....

feelings ....

MEANING

....

....

....

....

....

ACTION

....

....

....

8   importance ☆☆☆☆☆

Dream Description

date ....

....

....

....

....

....

....

....

....

....

....

....

....

....

....

....

....

....

....

....

....

....

....

Dream Tracker

Night Mind™
by bookmark™

title ....

date ....   recurring   ☐ Yes ☐ No

DAY BEFORE

events ....

food ....

dream seed™ ....

IN DREAM

my role ....

people ....

objects ....

events ....

feelings ....

MEANING

....

....

....

....

....

ACTION

....

....

....

importance ☆☆☆☆☆

Dream Description

date ....

....

....

....

....

....

....

....

....

....

....

....

....

....

....

....

....

....

....

....

....

....

....

....

....

....

....

Dream Tracker

title ....

date .... recurring ❑ Yes ❑ No

---

DAY BEFORE

events ....

food ....

dream seed™ ....

IN DREAM

my role ....

people ....

objects ....

events ....

feelings ....

MEANING

....

....

....

....

....

ACTION

....

....

....

12   importance ☆☆☆☆☆

Dream Description

date ....

....
....
....
....
....
....
....
....
....
....
....
....
....
....
....
....
....
....
....
....
....
....
....
....
....

Dream Tracker

Night Mind™
by **bookmark**™

title ....

date .... recurring ☐ Yes ☐ No

DAY BEFORE

events ....

food ....

dream seed™ ....

IN DREAM

my role ....

people ....

objects ....

events ....

feelings ....

MEANING

....

....

....

....

....

ACTION

....

....

....

14   importance ☆☆☆☆☆

Dream Description

date ....

....
....
....
....
....
....
....
....
....
....
....
....
....
....
....
....
....
....
....
....
....
....

Dream Tracker

title ....

date .... recurring ☐ Yes ☐ No

DAY BEFORE

events ....

food ....

dream seed™ ....

IN DREAM

my role ....

people ....

objects ....

events ....

feelings ....

MEANING

....

....

....

....

....

ACTION

....

....

....

16   importance ☆☆☆☆☆

Dream Description

date ....

....

....

....

....

....

....

....

....

....

....

....

....

....

....

....

....

....

....

....

....

....

....

Dream Tracker

title ....

date .... recurring ☐ Yes ☐ No

DAY BEFORE

events ....

food ....

dream seed™ ....

IN DREAM

my role ....

people ....

objects ....

events ....

feelings ....

MEANING

....

....

....

....

....

ACTION

....

....

....

18   importance ☆☆☆☆☆

Dream Description

date ....

....
....
....
....
....
....
....
....
....
....
....
....
....
....
....
....
....
....
....
....
....
....

Dream Tracker

title ....

date ....   recurring   ☐ Yes ☐ No

DAY BEFORE

events ....

food ....

dream seed™ ....

IN DREAM

my role ....

people ....

objects ....

events ....

feelings ....

MEANING

....

....

....

....

....

ACTION

....

....

....

20   importance ☆☆☆☆☆

Dream Description

Night Mind™
by bookmark™

date ....

....

....

....

....

....

....

....

....

....

....

....

....

....

....

....

....

....

....

....

....

....

....

....

Dream Tracker

Night Mind™
by bookmark™

title ....

date .... recurring ☐ Yes ☐ No

DAY BEFORE

events ....

food ....

dream seed™ ....

IN DREAM

my role ....

people ....

objects ....

events ....

feelings ....

MEANING

....

....

....

....

....

ACTION

....

....

....

importance ☆☆☆☆☆

Dream Description

date ....

....

....

....

....

....

....

....

....

....

....

....

....

....

....

....

....

....

....

....

....

....

....

....

....

Dream Tracker

title ....

date .... recurring ☐ Yes ☐ No

DAY BEFORE

events ....

food ....

dream seed™ ....

IN DREAM

my role ....

people ....

objects ....

events ....

feelings ....

MEANING

....

....

....

....

....

ACTION

....

....

....

importance ☆☆☆☆☆

Dream Description

date ....

....
....
....
....
....
....
....
....
....
....
....
....
....
....
....
....
....
....
....
....
....

Dream Tracker

Night Mind™
by bookmark™ [pro]

title ....

date .... recurring ❏ Yes ❏ No

DAY BEFORE

events ....

food ....

dream seed™ ....

IN DREAM

my role ....

people ....

objects ....

events ....

feelings ....

MEANING

....

....

....

....

....

ACTION

....

....

....

importance ☆☆☆☆☆

Dream Description

Night Mind™
by bookmark™

date ....

....
....
....
....
....
....
....
....
....
....
....
....
....
....
....
....
....
....
....
....
....
....
....

Dream Tracker

title ....

date ....   recurring   ☐ Yes ☐ No

DAY BEFORE

events ....

food ....

dream seed™ ....

IN DREAM

my role ....

people ....

objects ....

events ....

feelings ....

MEANING

....

....

....

....

....

ACTION

....

....

....

28   importance ☆☆☆☆☆

Dream Description

date ....

....

....

....

....

....

....

....

....

....

....

....

....

....

....

....

....

....

....

....

....

....

....

....

....

Dream Tracker

title ....

date .... recurring ☐ Yes ☐ No

DAY BEFORE

events ....

food ....

dream seed™ ....

IN DREAM

my role ....

people ....

objects ....

events ....

feelings ....

MEANING

....

....

....

....

....

ACTION

....

....

....

importance ☆☆☆☆☆

Dream Description

date ....

....

....

....

....

....

....

....

....

....

....

....

....

....

....

....

....

....

....

....

....

....

....

....

Dream Tracker

title ....

date .... recurring ☐ Yes ☐ No

DAY BEFORE

events ....

food ....

dream seed™ ....

IN DREAM

my role ....

people ....

objects ....

events ....

feelings ....

MEANING

....

....

....

....

....

ACTION

....

....

....

　　　　　importance ☆☆☆☆☆

Dream Description

date ....

....

....

....

....

....

....

....

....

....

....

....

....

....

....

....

....

....

....

....

....

....

....

....

Dream Tracker

Night Mind™
by bookmark™ pro

title ....

date ....   recurring   ☐ Yes ☐ No

DAY BEFORE

events ....

food ....

dream seed™ ....

IN DREAM

my role ....

people ....

objects ....

events ....

feelings ....

MEANING

....

....

....

....

....

ACTION

....

....

....

importance ☆☆☆☆☆

Dream Description

date ....

....

....

....

....

....

....

....

....

....

....

....

....

....

....

....

....

....

....

....

....

....

....

....

Dream Tracker

title ....

date .... recurring ☐ Yes ☐ No

DAY BEFORE

events ....

food ....

dream seed™ ....

IN DREAM

my role ....

people ....

objects ....

events ....

feelings ....

MEANING

....

....

....

....

....

ACTION

....

....

....

36   importance ☆☆☆☆☆

Dream Description

date ....

....

....

....

....

....

....

....

....

....

....

....

....

....

....

....

....

....

....

....

....

....

....

....

....

Dream Tracker

title ....

date .... recurring ☐ Yes ☐ No

DAY BEFORE

events ....

food ....

dream seed™ ....

IN DREAM

my role ....

people ....

objects ....

events ....

feelings ....

MEANING

....

....

....

....

....

ACTION

....

....

....

38   importance ☆☆☆☆☆

Dream Description

date ....

....

....

....

....

....

....

....

....

....

....

....

....

....

....

....

....

....

....

....

....

....

Dream Tracker

title ....

date .... recurring ☐ Yes ☐ No

---

DAY BEFORE

events ....

food ....

dream seed™ ....

IN DREAM

my role ....

people ....

objects ....

events ....

feelings ....

MEANING

....

....

....

....

....

ACTION

....

....

....

40   importance ☆☆☆☆☆

Dream Description

date ....

....

....

....

....

....

....

....

....

....

....

....

....

....

....

....

....

....

....

....

....

....

....

....

Dream Tracker

title ....

date .... recurring ☐ Yes ☐ No

DAY BEFORE

events ....

food ....

dream seed™ ....

IN DREAM

my role ....

people ....

objects ....

events ....

feelings ....

MEANING

....

....

....

....

....

ACTION

....

....

....

42   importance ☆☆☆☆☆

Dream Description

date ....

....

....

....

....

....

....

....

....

....

....

....

....

....

....

....

....

....

....

....

....

....

....

Dream Tracker

title ....

date .... recurring ☐ Yes ☐ No

DAY BEFORE

events ....

food ....

dream seed™ ....

IN DREAM

my role ....

people ....

objects ....

events ....

feelings ....

MEANING

....

....

....

....

....

ACTION

....

....

....

44   importance ☆☆☆☆☆

Dream Description

date ....

....

....

....

....

....

....

....

....

....

....

....

....

....

....

....

....

....

....

....

....

Dream Tracker

title ....

date .... recurring ☐ Yes ☐ No

DAY BEFORE

events ....

food ....

dream seed™ ....

IN DREAM

my role ....

people ....

objects ....

events ....

feelings ....

MEANING

....

....

....

....

....

ACTION

....

....

....

46 importance ☆☆☆☆☆

Dream Description

Night Mind™
by bookmark™

date ....

....

....

....

....

....

....

....

....

....

....

....

....

....

....

....

....

....

....

....

....

....

....

....

Dream Tracker

title ....

date .... recurring ☐ Yes ☐ No

DAY BEFORE

events ....

food ....

dream seed™ ....

IN DREAM

my role ....

people ....

objects ....

events ....

feelings ....

MEANING

....

....

....

....

....

ACTION

....

....

....

48   importance ☆☆☆☆☆

Dream Description

date ....

....

....

....

....

....

....

....

....

....

....

....

....

....

....

....

....

....

....

....

....

....

....

....

Dream Tracker

Night Mind™
by bookmark™ [pro]

title ....

date ....   recurring   ❐ Yes ❐ No

DAY BEFORE

events ....

food ....

dream seed™ ....

IN DREAM

my role ....

people ....

objects ....

events ....

feelings ....

MEANING

....

....

....

....

....

ACTION

....

....

....

       importance ☆☆☆☆☆

Recurring Dreams

1 ....

....

2 ....

....

3 ....

....

4 ....

....

5 ....

....

6 ....

....

7 ....

....

8 ....

....

9 ....

....

10 ....

....

11 ....

....

12 ....

....

Recurring Dreams

Night Mind™
by bookmark™

13...

14...

15...

16...

17...

18 ....

19 ....

20 ....

21..

22 ....

23 ....

24 ....

Dream Description

date ....

....

....

....

....

....

....

....

....

....

....

....

....

....

....

....

....

....

....

....

....

....

....

Dream Tracker

title ....

date .... recurring ☐ Yes ☐ No

DAY BEFORE

events ....

food ....

dream seed™ ....

IN DREAM

my role ....

people ....

objects ....

events ....

feelings ....

MEANING

....

....

....

....

....

ACTION

....

....

....

54   importance ☆☆☆☆☆

Dream Description

Night Mind™
by bookmark™ [pro]

date ....

....
....
....
....
....
....
....
....
....
....
....
....
....
....
....
....
....
....
....
....
....
....
....
....

55

Dream Tracker

Night Mind™
by bookmark™

title ....

date .... recurring ☐ Yes ☐ No

DAY BEFORE

events ....

food ....

dream seed™ ....

IN DREAM

my role ....

people ....

objects ....

events ....

feelings ....

MEANING

....

....

....

....

....

ACTION

....

....

....

importance ☆☆☆☆☆

Dream Description

date ....

....

....

....

....

....

....

....

....

....

....

....

....

....

....

....

....

....

....

....

....

....

Dream Tracker

title ....

date .... recurring ☐ Yes ☐ No

---

DAY BEFORE

events ....

food ....

dream seed™ ....

IN DREAM

my role ....

people ....

objects ....

events ....

feelings ....

MEANING

....

....

....

....

....

ACTION

....

....

....

importance ☆☆☆☆☆

Dream Description

Night Mind™
by bookmark™

date ....

....

....

....

....

....

....

....

....

....

....

....

....

....

....

....

....

....

....

....

....

Dream Tracker

Night Mind™
by bookmark™

title ....

date .... recurring ☐ Yes ☐ No

DAY BEFORE

events ....

food ....

dream seed™ ....

IN DREAM

my role ....

people ....

objects ....

events ....

feelings ....

MEANING

....

....

....

....

....

ACTION

....

....

....

60 importance ☆☆☆☆☆

Dream Description

date ....

....

....

....

....

....

....

....

....

....

....

....

....

....

....

....

....

....

....

....

....

....

....

Dream Tracker

title ....

date .... recurring ☐ Yes ☐ No

DAY BEFORE

events ....

food ....

dream seed™ ....

IN DREAM

my role ....

people ....

objects ....

events ....

feelings ....

MEANING

....

....

....

....

....

ACTION

....

....

....

importance ☆☆☆☆☆

Dream Description

date ....

....

....

....

....

....

....

....

....

....

....

....

....

....

....

....

....

....

....

....

....

....

....

Dream Tracker

title ....

date .... recurring ☐ Yes ☐ No

DAY BEFORE

events ....

food ....

dream seed™ ....

IN DREAM

my role ....

people ....

objects ....

events ....

feelings ....

MEANING

....

....

....

....

....

ACTION

....

....

....

64   importance ☆☆☆☆☆

Dream Description

date ....

....
....
....
....
....
....
....
....
....
....
....
....
....
....
....
....
....
....
....
....
....
....
....

Dream Tracker

title ....

date .... recurring ☐ Yes ☐ No

DAY BEFORE

events ....

food ....

dream seed™ ....

IN DREAM

my role ....

people ....

objects ....

events ....

feelings ....

MEANING

....

....

....

....

....

ACTION

....

....

....

importance ☆☆☆☆☆

Dream Description

date ....

....

....

....

....

....

....

....

....

....

....

....

....

....

....

....

....

....

....

....

....

....

....

....

....

Dream Tracker

title ....

date .... recurring ☐ Yes ☐ No

DAY BEFORE

events ....

food ....

dream seed™ ....

IN DREAM

my role ....

people ....

objects ....

events ....

feelings ....

MEANING

....

....

....

....

....

ACTION

....

....

....

importance ☆☆☆☆☆

Dream Description

Night Mind™
by bookmark™

date ....

....
....
....
....
....
....
....
....
....
....
....
....
....
....
....
....
....
....
....
....
....
....
....
....

Dream Tracker

title ....

date .... recurring ☐ Yes ☐ No

DAY BEFORE

events ....

food ....

dream seed™ ....

IN DREAM

my role ....

people ....

objects ....

events ....

feelings ....

MEANING

....

....

....

....

....

ACTION

....

....

....

importance ☆☆☆☆☆

Dream Description

date ....

....

....

....

....

....

....

....

....

....

....

....

....

....

....

....

....

....

....

....

....

....

....

....

....

Dream Tracker

title ....

date .... recurring ☐ Yes ☐ No

---

DAY BEFORE

events ....

food ....

dream seed™ ....

IN DREAM

my role ....

people ....

objects ....

events ....

feelings ....

MEANING

....

....

....

....

....

ACTION

....

....

....

72   importance ☆☆☆☆☆

Dream Description

date ....

....

....

....

....

....

....

....

....

....

....

....

....

....

....

....

....

....

....

....

....

....

....

....

....

Dream Tracker

title ....

date .... recurring ☐ Yes ☐ No

DAY BEFORE

events ....

food ....

dream seed™ ....

IN DREAM

my role ....

people ....

objects ....

events ....

feelings ....

MEANING

....

....

....

....

....

ACTION

....

....

....

74   importance ☆☆☆☆☆

Dream Description

date ....

....

....

....

....

....

....

....

....

....

....

....

....

....

....

....

....

....

....

....

....

....

....

....

Dream Tracker

title ....

date .... recurring ☐ Yes ☐ No

DAY BEFORE

events ....

food ....

dream seed™ ....

IN DREAM

my role ....

people ....

objects ....

events ....

feelings ....

MEANING

....

....

....

....

....

ACTION

....

....

....

76   importance ☆☆☆☆☆

Dream Description

date ....

....

....

....

....

....

....

....

....

....

....

....

....

....

....

....

....

....

....

....

....

....

....

Dream Tracker

title ....

date .... recurring ☐ Yes ☐ No

DAY BEFORE

events ....

food ....

dream seed™ ....

IN DREAM

my role ....

people ....

objects ....

events ....

feelings ....

MEANING

....

....

....

....

....

ACTION

....

....

....

78   importance ☆☆☆☆☆

Dream Description

date ....

....

....

....

....

....

....

....

....

....

....

....

....

....

....

....

....

....

....

....

....

....

Dream Tracker

title ....

date ....   recurring   ☐ Yes ☐ No

DAY BEFORE

events ....

food ....

dream seed™ ....

IN DREAM

my role ....

people ....

objects ....

events ....

feelings ....

MEANING

....

....

....

....

....

ACTION

....

....

....

80   importance ☆☆☆☆☆

Dream Description

date ....

....

....

....

....

....

....

....

....

....

....

....

....

....

....

....

....

....

....

....

....

....

....

Dream Tracker

Night Mind™
by bookmark™ [pro]

title ....

date .... recurring ☐ Yes ☐ No

DAY BEFORE

events ....

food ....

dream seed™ ....

IN DREAM

my role ....

people ....

objects ....

events ....

feelings ....

MEANING

....

....

....

....

....

ACTION

....

....

....

82   importance ☆☆☆☆☆

Dream Description

Night Mind™
by pro bookmark™

date ....

....

....

....

....

....

....

....

....

....

....

....

....

....

....

....

....

....

....

....

....

....

....

....

Dream Tracker

title ....

date .... recurring ☐ Yes ☐ No

DAY BEFORE

events ....

food ....

dream seed™ ....

IN DREAM

my role ....

people ....

objects ....

events ....

feelings ....

MEANING

....

....

....

....

....

ACTION

....

....

....

84 importance ☆☆☆☆☆

Dream Description

Night Mind™
by bookmark™

date ....

....

....

....

....

....

....

....

....

....

....

....

....

....

....

....

....

....

....

....

....

....

....

Dream Tracker

title ....

date .... recurring ☐ Yes ☐ No

DAY BEFORE

events ....

food ....

dream seed™ ....

IN DREAM

my role ....

people ....

objects ....

events ....

feelings ....

MEANING

....

....

....

....

....

ACTION

....

....

....

importance ☆☆☆☆☆

Dream Description

date ....

....

....

....

....

....

....

....

....

....

....

....

....

....

....

....

....

....

....

....

....

....

....

Dream Tracker

title ....

date .... recurring ☐ Yes ☐ No

DAY BEFORE

events ....

food ....

dream seed™ ....

IN DREAM

my role ....

people ....

objects ....

events ....

feelings ....

MEANING

....

....

....

....

....

ACTION

....

....

....

88   importance ☆☆☆☆☆

Dream Description

date ....

....

....

....

....

....

....

....

....

....

....

....

....

....

....

....

....

....

....

....

....

....

....

....

Dream Tracker

title ....

date ....   recurring   ☐ Yes ☐ No

DAY BEFORE

events ....

food ....

dream seed™ ....

IN DREAM

my role ....

people ....

objects ....

events ....

feelings ....

MEANING

....

....

....

....

....

ACTION

....

....

....

90   importance ☆☆☆☆☆

Dream Description

date ....

....

....

....

....

....

....

....

....

....

....

....

....

....

....

....

....

....

....

....

....

....

....

Dream Tracker

Night Mind™
by bookmark™ pro

title ....

date .... recurring ☐ Yes ☐ No

DAY BEFORE

events ....

food ....

dream seed™ ....

IN DREAM

my role ....

people ....

objects ....

events ....

feelings ....

MEANING

....

....

....

....

....

ACTION

....

....

....

importance ☆☆☆☆☆

Dream Description

date ....

....

....

....

....

....

....

....

....

....

....

....

....

....

....

....

....

....

....

....

....

....

....

....

....

Dream Tracker

Night Mind™
by bookmark™ [pro]

title ....

date .... recurring ☐ Yes ☐ No

DAY BEFORE

events ....

food ....

dream seed™ ....

IN DREAM

my role ....

people ....

objects ....

events ....

feelings ....

MEANING

....

....

....

....

....

ACTION

....

....

....

94   importance ☆☆☆☆☆

Dream Description

date ....

....

....

....

....

....

....

....

....

....

....

....

....

....

....

....

....

....

....

....

....

....

....

....

Dream Tracker

title ....

date .... recurring ☐ Yes ☐ No

---

DAY BEFORE

events ....

food ....

dream seed™ ....

IN DREAM

my role ....

people ....

objects ....

events ....

feelings ....

MEANING

....

....

....

....

....

ACTION

....

....

....

96   importance ☆☆☆☆☆

Dream Description

Night Mind™
by bookmark™

date ....

Dream Tracker

title ....

date .... recurring ❐ Yes ❐ No

DAY BEFORE

events ....

food ....

dream seed™ ....

IN DREAM

my role ....

people ....

objects ....

events ....

feelings ....

MEANING

....

....

....

....

....

ACTION

....

....

....

98   importance ☆☆☆☆☆

Dream Description

date ....

....

....

....

....

....

....

....

....

....

....

....

....

....

....

....

....

....

....

....

....

....

....

....

....

Dream Tracker

Night Mind™
by **bookmark**™

title ....

date .... recurring ☐ Yes ☐ No

DAY BEFORE

events ....

food ....

dream seed™ ....

IN DREAM

my role ....

people ....

objects ....

events ....

feelings ....

MEANING

....

....

....

....

....

ACTION

....

....

....

100   importance ☆☆☆☆☆

Dream Description

date ....

....

....

....

....

....

....

....

....

....

....

....

....

....

....

....

....

....

....

....

....

....

....

Dream Tracker

title ....

date ....   recurring   ❏ Yes ❏ No

---

DAY BEFORE

events ....

food ....

dream seed™ ....

IN DREAM

my role ....

people ....

objects ....

events ....

feelings ....

MEANING

....

....

....

....

....

ACTION

....

....

....

102   importance ☆☆☆☆☆

Recurring Dreams

1 ....

....

2 ....

....

3 ....

....

4 ....

....

5 ....

....

6 ....

....

7 ....

....

8 ....

....

9 ....

....

10 ....

....

11 ....

....

12 ....

....

Recurring Dreams

13..

....

14..

....

15..

....

16..

....

17..

....

18..

....

19..

....

20..

....

21..

....

22..

....

23..

....

24..

....